VIEWS

SEATTLE AND THE PUGET SOUND

EMERALD POINT PRESS

an imprint of

ISBN 10: 0-9637816-1-8
ISBN 13: 978-0-9637816-1-1

Copyright © 2006
Thunder Bay Press, Holt, Michigan

Copyright © 2002
Emerald Point Press, Seattle, Washington
An imprint of Thunder Bay Press

Library of Congress Catalog Card Number 95-60449

Printed in China

It is the artists interpretation of reality, that help us view life, in perspectives that we otherwise may not see. These views of Seattle and the Puget Sound, were all produced by Seattle area photographers. These seasonal images, capture forever, that moment in time, when all forces necessary to create perfection converge.

The city and landscape photographs reproduced in this book, were created by: Bill Brooksher, Dan Carow, John S. Chao, Adrienne DeLiso, Joe Faulkner, Neal Herbert, Chris Jacobson, S.H. Marti, Joe Poehlman, and John Rizzo.

Their artistic vision is yours to enjoy.

▲

South of Ruby Beach—Olympic National Park Seashore

Adrienne DeLiso

John S. Chao

TULIP FIELDS—SKAGIT VALLEY

Mount Shuksan viewed from Picture Lake—Mount Baker Wilderness

Chris Jacobson

WAHKEENA FALLS—COLUMBIA RIVER GORGE

Chris Jacobson

Wooden Boats on Lake Union

Chris Jacobson

Joe Poehlman

SEATTLE VIEWED FROM LAKE UNION

Chris Jacobson

Chris Jacobson

Mount Shuksan–Mount Baker Wilderness

John S. Chao

FRANKLIN FALLS IN WINTER—SNOQUALMIE PASS

SEATTLE AT DUSK VIEWED FROM THE SOUTH

Joe Poehlman

VIEW FROM HURRICANE RIDGE—OLYMPIC NATIONAL PARK

Dan Carou

Chris Jacobson

SNOW LAKE—MOUNT RAINIER NATIONAL PARK

Chris Jacobson

Adrienne DeLiso

SEATTLE VIEWED FROM WEST SEATTLE

Bill Brooksher

Bill Brooksher

SEATTLE VIEWED FROM LAKE UNION

FISHERMAN'S TERMINAL—SEATTLE

Chris Jacobson

MOONRISE IN SEATTLE FROM MAGNOLIA PARK

Chris Jacobson

Chris Jacobson

POINT WILSON LIGHTHOUSE
FORT WORDEN STATE PARK

Adrienne DeLiso

Joe Faulkner

EDMONDS FERRY AND OLYMPIC MOUNTAINS

Joe Poehlma

John S. Chao

SOURCE LAKE STREAM—SNOQUALMIE PASS

FIREWORKS OVER LAKE UNION

S.H. Mart

Chris Jacobson

TULIP GARDENS—MOUNT VERNON

SEA STACKS
OLYMPIC NATIONAL PARK
SEASHORE

Neal Herbert

Bill Brooksher

KUBOTA GARDENS IN AUTUMN

Bill Brooksher

Bill Brooksher

NORTH HEAD LIGHTHOUSE—COLUMBIA RIVER

S.H. Mart

Chris Jacobson

MOUNT RAINIER VIEWED FROM REFLECTION LAKES—MOUNT RAINIER NATIONAL PARK

WINTER EVENING IN SEATTLE VIEWED FROM QUEEN ANNE HILL

Bill Brooksher

MOUNT RAINIER VIEWED FROM REFLECTION LAKES–MOUNT RAINIER NATIONAL PARK

VIEW FROM MAGNOLIA PARK

Joe Faulkner

FALLS CREEK FALLS NEAR OHANAPECOSH
MOUNT RAINIER NATIONAL PARK

Chris Jacobson

FALL LEAVES—WASHINGTON PARK ARBORETUM

Chris Jacobson

PINNACLE PEAK–MOUNT RAINIER NATIONAL PARK

JAPANESE GARDEN—WASHINGTON PARK ARBORETUM

Joe Poehlman

Chris Jacobson

FISHERMAN'S TERMINAL—SEATTLE

Bill Brooksher

TULIP GARDENS
MOUNT VERNON

Chris Jacobson

MOUNT SHUKSAN IN WINTER VIEWED FROM PICTURE LAKE—MOUNT BAKER WILDERNESS

S.H. Marti

H. Marti

MOUNT SHUKSAN IN FALL VIEWED FROM PICTURE LAKE—MOUNT BAKER WILDERNESS

RUBY BEACH—OLYMPIC NATIONAL PARK SEASHORE

Bill Brookshe

CRYSTAL FALLS
MOUNT RAINIER NATIONAL PARK

Chris Jacobson

Seattle viewed from Kerry Park on Queen Anne Hill

Chris Jacobson

5

Adrienne DeLiso

EBEY'S LANDING—WHIDBEY ISLAND

Joe Poehlman

Chris Jacobson

SEATTLE VIEWED FROM HARBOR ISLAND

S.H. Mart

Chris Jacobson

JAPANESE GARDEN—WASHINGTON PARK ARBORETUM

Mount Rainier viewed from the Snow Lake Trail—Mount Rainier National Park

Chris Jacobson

HOH RAIN FOREST
OLYMPIC NATIONAL PARK

Neal Herbert

Fishing Boat—Gig Harbor

Chris Jacobson

S.H. Marti

Sea Stacks—North Rialto Beach—Olympic National Park Seashore

SEATTLE AT SUNSET VIEWED FROM WEST SEATTLE

Bill Brookshe

John Rizzo